HOW TO DRAW
ENDANGERED ANIMALS

by
Molly Walsh

illustrated by
Bob Pepper

Produced by Jump Start Press

ISBN 0-8167-5034-3
10 9 8 7 6 5 4 3 2 1

SAVE THE ANIMALS

Endangered animals are at great risk of becoming extinct. When an animal becomes extinct, it is no longer living anywhere on Earth. Ninety-nine percent of all the species that have ever existed are now extinct!

Even though some animals become endangered or extinct due to natural causes—such as climate changes, volcanoes, or disease—people are more often the biggest threat. Humans can and do live just about everywhere on Earth. Unfortunately, the story is not the same for animals. Every species has a habitat, or special home, where it is best able to survive. Habitat loss is the most common threat to animals. As the human population grows, people take up land where animals once roamed free. Former animal habitats are now farms, pastures, ranch land, and new neighborhoods.

Pollution is another threat. Many animals are suffering from the effects of all the chemicals and waste that people produce. People have created disasters ranging from oil spills to the spread of poisons that are harmful to animals.

In addition, humans sometimes compete with animals for food and kill wild animals to protect their land and livestock. People also hunt many animals for sport and money.

But there is hope. The 1972 Endangered Species Act is a law that makes it illegal to harm species on the endangered list in any way. There are also many zoos, all over the world, that raise endangered animals and try to release the young back into the wild, in the hope that the species will be able to grow and thrive once again on its own.

You can help too. Taking care of the environment is a good place to start. Reuse and recycle paper and plastics. If everyone in the world recycled newspapers, 500,000 trees would be saved each week. That would preserve a lot of animal habitats. Take care of habitats near where you live by not littering. If you see litter, pick it up and throw it away properly. And always respect the living things around you. That means giving wild animals their space and not disturbing their homes.

Many zoos have "Adopt an Endangered Animal" programs. They give you lots of information on your animal, so that you can learn how to help save the species. The programs can cost some money, so you may want to try to get your class or a group of friends involved. The money you send goes into a special fund to help protect the animal you adopt.

We must realize that all animals depend on one another for survival. Any time a species becomes extinct, it affects everyone. We should all try to do what we can to help protect the animals. And who knows? If we work together, maybe the animals you're drawing from this book will one day be out of danger!

READY, SET, DRAW!

Get ready to explore the wild world of endangered animals. This book will show you how to draw these amazing creatures step by step.

To begin, you will need a #2 lead pencil, a soft drafting pencil for shading, and a good eraser. Erasers that can be kneaded to get at tiny lines work especially well. Be sure to keep a pencil sharpener nearby and use it often so your lines don't get smudgy.

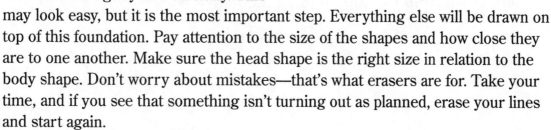

soft drafting pencil

#2 lead pencil

pencil sharpener

kneaded eraser

Step 1 will always ask you to draw the basic shapes of the animal. Sketch the first lines lightly and carefully. This may look easy, but it is the most important step. Everything else will be drawn on top of this foundation. Pay attention to the size of the shapes and how close they are to one another. Make sure the head shape is the right size in relation to the body shape. Don't worry about mistakes—that's what erasers are for. Take your time, and if you see that something isn't turning out as planned, erase your lines and start again.

In the next steps you will refine your basic shapes. Don't be concerned with the details until the end.

Keep your lines light until the animal's shape is complete. Now you can add details, such as fur and feathers. Some animals have very distinct patterns. Look closely at these markings and try to repeat them all over the body.

The last step is to shade body parts to make them look realistic and add dimension to your drawing. Think about the real animal. Notice how some of your guidelines can help you see how the animal moves. Pay attention to where each animal's joints and muscles are. When body parts overlap, make the lines darker to show separation. Also darken areas that are farther away. Be sure to erase any extra lines or markings you don't need. Finally, you can add colors to your finished animals, if you'd like.

The most important thing is to relax and have fun with your drawing. You probably won't get it just right on your first try. It will take some practice. But if you keep at it, soon you'll be drawing animals that look like they came straight from the wild!

BLUE WHALE

Blue whales are the largest creatures on Earth today. They can grow up to 100 feet long. That's even bigger than the largest dinosaur! Blue whales are endangered because people have hunted and killed too many of them and have polluted the oceans where they live.

 **STEP 1**
Draw a basic oval shape for the body. Sketch a curved line up from the bottom of the oval, to form the mouth, and another one down from the top, to form the tail.

 STEP 2
Draw a banana-shaped line across the top of the oval, from the end of the mouth line to the end of the tail. Continue the other side of the "banana" about halfway through the oval. Near the bottom of the oval, curve the line slightly up to make the mouth. Position the eye at the bottom of the oval.

 4

STEP 3

Add triangular shapes for the flipper and the tail fins, a lump to the top of the head, and a small fin to the top of the tail. Sketch a line above and parallel to the first mouth line, and another above the flipper. Draw curved lines on the underside of the whale, from the mouth lines to midway down the body.

STEP 4

Now it's time to add the final details. Shade in the area directly underneath the tail and around the mouth. Leave the lined underside a lighter color. Complete the whale by adding some spots on its back. Be sure to erase any unwanted lines. Congratulations—you've just drawn your first endangered species!

WEST INDIAN MANATEE

Manatees live in coastal areas, mainly in Florida. They can grow to be 10 feet long and weigh up to 1,000 pounds. Many manatee deaths are related to people. Causes include pollution, collisions with boats, and building in the manatee's habitat. To protect manatees, laws have been passed enforcing speed zones for boats and making certain waterways off-limits to people.

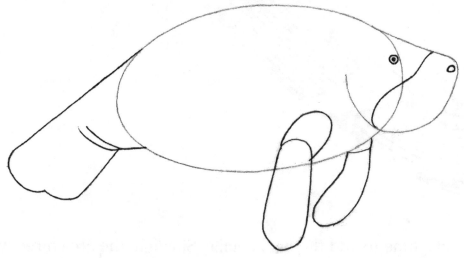

 STEP 1 Draw a simple oval shape for the body. Add a line starting at the top of the oval, and curve it back into the oval so it makes a half circle. This will be your manatee's head.

 STEP 2 Add the flippers and the tail, as shown. Next, draw a nostril, a snout, and an eye. Don't forget to include the pupil in the center of the eye.

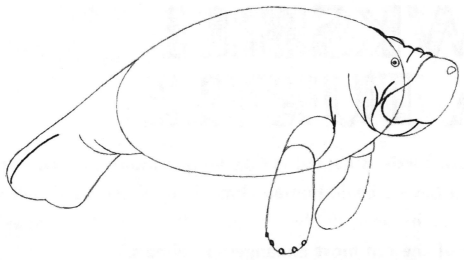

Add the mouth lines to the bottom of the snout. Then add wrinkles to the neck and forehead. Draw small fingernails on the front flipper. Sketch a contour line on the tail.

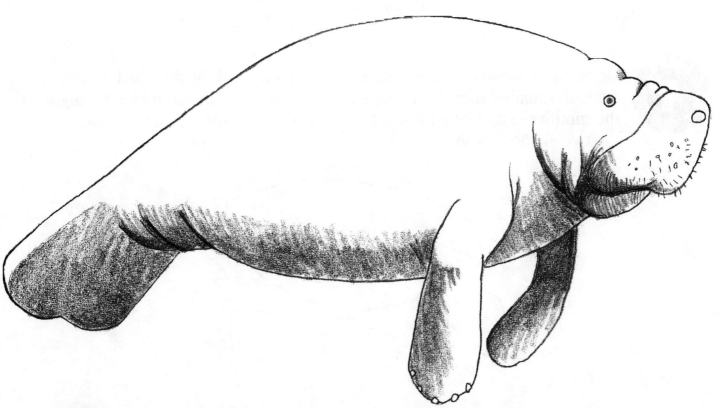

Add some shading around the lines of the face. Draw small lines for whiskers on the snout. Shade in the underside of the body, the inside of the flippers, and the tail. Erase any extra lines, and your manatee is all set to swim.

HAWKSBILL SEA TURTLE

The hawksbill sea turtle is named for its unique mouth, which hooks downward like a hawk's beak. Humans have hunted the hawksbill sea turtle so much for its beautiful brown-and-yellow shell that today it is considered one of the ten most endangered animals.

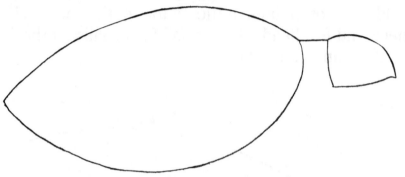

 Draw an oval-shaped outline with a point at one end for the shell. Sketch a small, rounded triangular shape for the head. Be sure to make the tip of the mouth pointy like a hawk's beak. Now draw a short line to connect the two shapes, as shown.

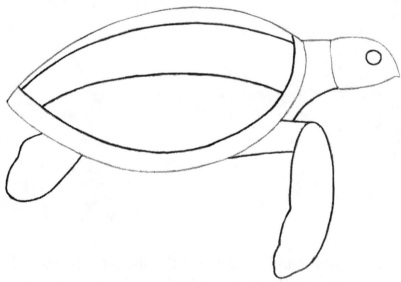

 Sketch the outlines for the front flipper and back flipper. Draw guidelines on the shell, as shown. This will help you position the turtle's markings in step 3. Add a line to form the bottom of the neck. Remember to include a circle for the eye.

8

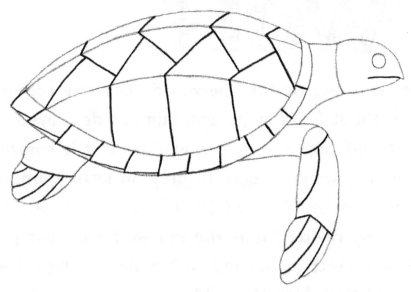

STEP 3 Start adding markings on the shell using straight lines to form triangles and rectangles, as shown. Lightly draw guidelines on the flippers. Add a line for the mouth.

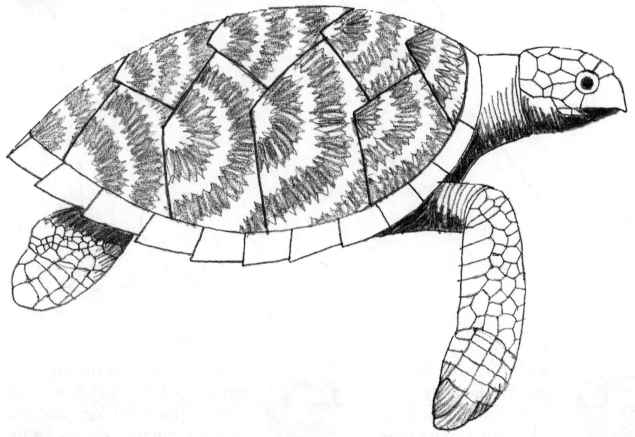

STEP 4 Using the guidelines from step 3, add detail to the flippers and head to make the turtle look scaly. Draw the delicate pattern on the shell, as shown. Shade the underside of the neck and flippers, and darken the pupil. Erase any extra pencil lines. Do you think you might add colors to your turtle?

RED WOLF

The red wolf is the smallest wolf in the world. Its name comes from its reddish-colored fur. About forty years ago, humans destroyed most of the red wolf's habitat by putting up lots of buildings in the southeastern United States. When red wolves began to prey on farm animals, programs to protect the farm animals killed off 50,000 red wolves within thirty years. People eventually realized that the red wolf was nearly extinct, and laws were passed to protect it. The red wolf is now being raised in captivity and released back into the wild.

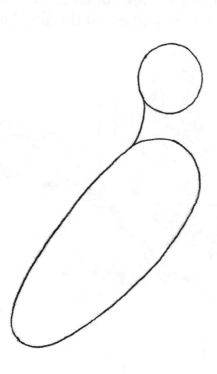

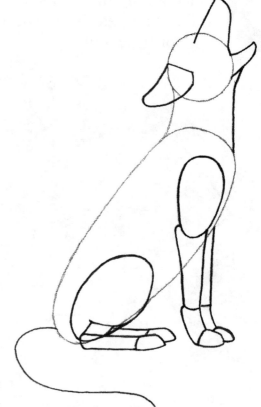

Start by drawing an oval shape for the body, making it narrower toward the bottom. Draw a circle for the head near the top of the body. Connect the head and the body with a short line, as shown.

Draw two ovals for the upper part of the legs. Sketch straight lines for the lower legs, and draw curved triangular shapes for the paws. Now add the howling snout, beginning at the top of the head. Draw a line to connect the chin to the chest. Begin to outline the ear and the tail.

STEP 3

Add the facial details, including a small black oval for the eye and a curved line for the tip of the nose. Complete the mouth and ear, as well. Be sure to add the line details to the face, as shown. This will help you fill in the shaded areas in step 4. Now is a good time to start outlining your wolf's furry coat. Fill out the tail by following the line you drew in step 2. Overlap lines a bit to show the roundness of the tail, and make the tip furry. Draw small lines to add detail to the paws.

STEP 4

Darken the nose, mouth, and ear. Continue adding the fur details, and fill in the shaded areas, as shown. Erase any unwanted lines, and your wolf is ready to howl!

KOMODO DRAGON

The Komodo dragon is the largest lizard in the world. The biggest Komodo dragon ever found was 10 feet long! It lives only on the island of Komodo and a few other islands north of Australia. Threats to its survival include illegal hunting and loss of habitat due to human settlement.

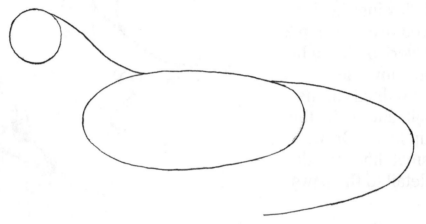

STEP 1 Start with an oval shape for the body. Then draw a small circle for the head. Connect the body and head with a curving line, as shown. Now add a sweeping line from the back of the body to begin the tail.

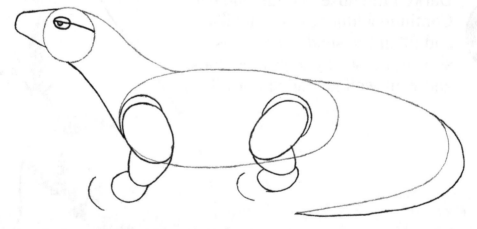

STEP 2 Draw oval shapes tilted in opposite directions at the front and back of the body for the top part of the legs. Add a curved line above each of the ovals. Sketch smaller shapes for the middle and lower legs and feet, as shown. Include two curved lines to position the claws. Add an eye, a snout, and a line for the underside of the neck. Draw a curved line starting about halfway down the tail to form a banana shape.

12

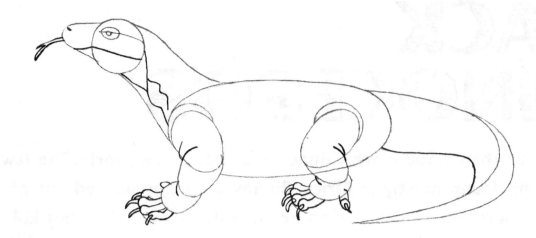

STEP 3

Carefully draw in the details on the the feet, including the claws. Add wrinkle lines around the leg joints. Complete the tail by drawing a curved line from the end of the body to the center of the banana shape. Outline the forked tongue, and add the nostril. Begin the mouth line on the underside of the snout, and add some wavy lines down the neck.

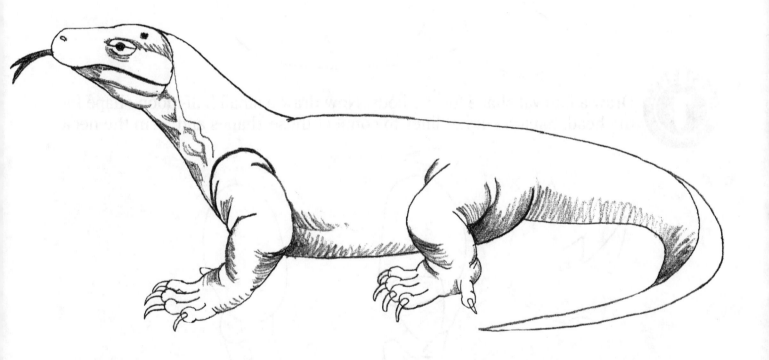

STEP 4

Add the finishing details to the feet and head, including shading the tongue, mouth, and eye. Shade in the areas around the leg joints and the underside of the belly and tail. Don't forget to add shading around the lines you drew on the neck to show the bulging veins. Erase any extra pencil lines, and your awesome dragon is complete!

BLACK RHINOCEROS

There are fewer than 3,500 black rhinoceroses left in the world. The few that remain are found mostly in Africa. Rhinos are being hunted out of existence. Poachers (hunters who trap or kill wild animals illegally) kill rhinos because they can sell their horns for a lot of money. Now wildlife officials saw off many rhino horns so the poachers have no reason to kill the rhinos.

 Draw a fat oval shape for the body. Now draw a small half-moon shape for the head. Sketch curved lines to connect these shapes and form the neck.

 Draw an upright oval on the back end of the body and another right behind the neck. Below each oval, draw two legs in three sections each: the thigh, the calf, and the hoof. Add two triangular shapes on top of the head for the horns, along with the ear, eye, and mouth.

 STEP 3 Round out the body by connecting all the parts to each other. Don't forget the small bump on the back. Draw some wrinkle lines on the neck, legs, and head. Give the facial features more detail. Draw toes on the hooves, and add a thin tail halfway down the rear of the body.

 STEP 4 Shade the underside of the body and the legs. Make the far legs a little darker. Add some more shading around the head area. Give definition to the horns and neck wrinkles by shading around them too. Darken the nostril, pupil, and tail. Erase any unwanted lines, and your rhino is all set to roam!

GRIZZLY BEAR

Grizzlies are among the world's largest bears. They can stand up to 8 feet tall and weigh half a ton! To live, they need lots of space in the wilderness. As people move into their habitat, the grizzlies must seek out more remote places. Grizzlies are also thought to be dangerous, so people sometimes kill them out of fear.

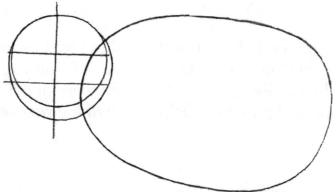

Draw a wide oval for the body. Next, draw a circle for the head that overlaps the body shape. Draw a half-circle inside the head shape. Lightly sketch three guidelines on the head to help you position the eyes, snout, and mouth in step 2.

Sketch a large oval for the shoulder and another one for the hind leg. Draw the wide sections of the lower legs, and add curved lines for the paws. Begin adding facial details, using the lines drawn in the head circle as a guide. Draw the eyes on the top horizontal line, as shown. Add the snout and the mouth along the guidelines—and don't forget to outline the ears.

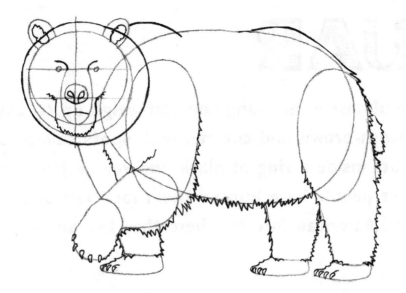

STEP 3 Draw another circle around the outside of the head. Add details to the ears and face, as shown. Draw bumps on the back—one by the neck and one by the hindquarters. Now it's time to add fur along the body. Don't forget to include a little, furry tail. Complete the feet, and draw claws on the paws.

STEP 4 Continue to make the body look furry. Darken the eye and mouth area, and fill in the nose and inner ears. Shade in the bear's belly, legs, and tail. Be sure to erase any extra pencil lines, and your grizzly is ready to roar!

JAGUAR

These big cats are almost 4 feet long and can weigh up to 250 pounds. Their coat is yellowish-brown and covered with spots called rosettes, which are solid black spots inside a ring of black and yellow. Jaguars are endangered because people have hunted them for their beautiful fur and because the Central American forests where they live are being destroyed.

STEP 1 Begin by sketching an oval body shape. Next, draw a circle near the body; this will be the head. Lightly sketch three guidelines on the head circle. Draw a neck line to connect the head circle to the body. Outline the tail with a smooth, curved line.

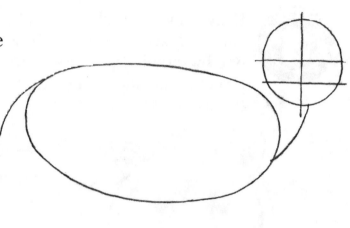

STEP 2 Draw ovals for the upper section of the legs. Sketch rectangular shapes for the lower legs, and draw curved lines to begin the paws. Pay attention to the angles of the leg joints. Now draw a line to define the top part of the neck, once again connecting the head circle to the body. Use the guidelines to help you add the facial details, including the eyes, nose, snout, and mouth— and don't forget to outline the ears.

STEP 3

Continue adding facial details. Soften the outline of the outer ears so they look furry, and draw the inner ears. Add the outline around the eyes. Fill in the tip of the nose, and add wrinkles to the neck with three curved lines. Smooth out the leg outlines. Add details to the paws, and finish the tail outline.

STEP 4

Darken the inner ears, the pupils, the nose, and the mouth. Add the spots on the muzzle. Shade the neck, the far legs, the belly, and the end of the tail. Take your time with the jaguar's coat, when drawing the rosettes on the body. Notice that the spots on the face and tail look more oval than round, and the spots get smaller on the legs and feet. Don't forget to include claws on the paws. Erase any unwanted lines, and your jaguar looks as if he could leap off the page!

19

SPOTTED OWL

The spotted owl is less than 2 feet tall and weighs only about 2 pounds. It was listed as endangered in 1989. To protect the spotted owl, the government has banned the cutting of trees where it lives on the western coast of America. This angered many workers who rely on the lumber industry in that area for jobs. But environmentalists say that this is the only way to save the spotted owl from extinction.

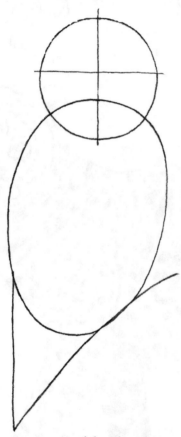

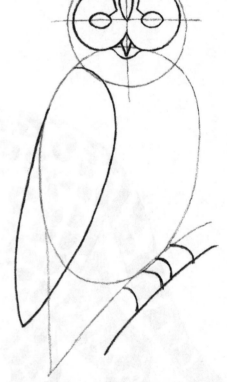

STEP 1

Draw an oval body shape. Now draw a head circle that overlaps the top of the body, and add two crossed guidelines inside the head circle. Draw a triangle shape for a tail, but continue one side of it out beyond the body shape. This will become a tree branch.

STEP 2

Center the eyes along the horizontal guideline. Lightly draw the inner and outer lines for the eyes. Draw a triangle beak, with a curved line beneath it. Next, draw an oval, but make the bottom end pointed. This will be the wing. Sketch a line for the bottom of the tree branch, and add the outlines of the feet.

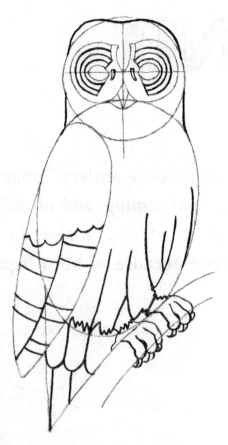

STEP 3

Add three half-circles around each inner eye, using the guidelines, and two small curved shapes between the eyes. Draw lines to connect the sides of the head to the body, and flatten out the top of the head. Then draw guidelines for the feather pattern, as shown. Carefully add details to the feet, including the claws.

STEP 4

It's time to complete the details. Darken the eyes and mouth. Blacken the owl's wing and head, leaving white spots, as shown. Shade in the feather pattern using the guidelines on the tail and belly. Make soft, short strokes with your pencil to create a feathery texture. Don't forget the area below the neck and around the eyes. Erase any extra pencil lines, and your owl is on the lookout!

WOODLAND CARIBOU

Woodland caribou are large animals with magnificent antlers. Today fewer than 7,000 woodland caribou exist. Logging, coal mining, and oil drilling have almost completely destroyed their habitat, which is mainly in Canada. In the past, caribou have also suffered because of both legal and illegal hunting.

 Draw a large oval for the body and a smaller oval for the head. Add a squared snout to the head. With a smooth motion, lightly sketch a curved guideline to position the antlers. Then draw three lines for the main antlers, as shown.

 Carefully outline the three antlers. This is the toughest part, so draw the lines slowly and lightly. Don't worry if they don't look exactly like the drawing here; you'll be able to perfect them in the next two steps. Sketch an ear at the base of the antlers, and add a small circle to position the eye. Draw a neck line from the bottom of the head to the body, and another from the top of the head. Now it's time to add the legs. Begin by drawing two oval shapes for the upper legs, then sketch the lower sections for all four legs and outline the hooves.

Now add the antlers on the far side, as shown. Draw the facial details. Add some wrinkles to the neck and body, and some fur on the chest. Smooth out the outline of the front leg. Be sure to include the detail on the hooves and a short tail.

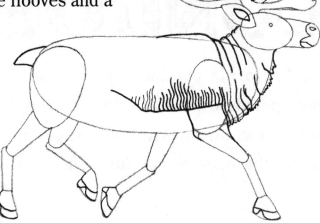

Add shading all over, as shown. Leave the chest area and tail white. Don't forget to darken the inner ear, eye, nostril, and hooves. Erase any unwanted lines, and your beautiful caribou is on the run!

CALIFORNIA CONDOR

The California condor is the world's largest vulture. It has been on Earth since prehistoric times. But as people settled the land, they took over the bird's food and nesting areas, pushing the condor toward extinction. Today, the only remaining condors live in captivity.

 Draw an egg shape for the body and a small circle for the head. Sketch a curved line for the beak. Outline a drumstick shape for the leg closest to you, and draw a small rectangle for the far leg. Now sketch a fan shape for the tail.

 Add a small circle for the eye, and draw a curved line to outline the bottom of the beak and the mouth. Sketch a curved line to form a banana shape on the top of the body for the neck feathers. Then draw curved lines from the head to the body to form the neck. For the wing, draw an oval with a flat end that overlaps the body. Carefully begin to outline the lower legs and feet.

24

STEP 3

Now you can start to add the feathers. Sketch spiky lines on the bottom of the wing and tail and on the chest and neck ruff. Draw guidelines across the wing to help shade in the feathers, as shown. Add detail lines to the beak, and complete the feet, including the claws. Also add a dot on the side of the face as part of the condor's unique markings.

STEP 4

Darken the beak, eye, ruff, chest, and tail feathers, and use the lines you drew in step 3 as guides for filling in the feather patterns on the wing. Lightly shade in the feet, and erase any extra pencil lines. Now your condor is ready to soar!

MOUNTAIN GORILLA

The mountain gorilla is the largest member of the ape family. These apes live in the mountain jungles of Africa. There are fewer than 400 mountain gorillas living in the wild today. Poaching and wars are the biggest threats to their existence. Many gorillas are now raised in captivity.

STEP 1 Draw a large jelly-bean shape for the body at the angle shown. Sketch an oval head that overlaps the body shape. Add guidelines on the head to help you draw the facial details.

STEP 2 Carefully position the arms and legs on the body. First draw an oval shape for the upper arm closest to you, then use rectangular shapes to outline the remaining parts of the arms and legs. Also begin to form the hands and feet, as shown. Use the guidelines to position the eyes and mouth. Draw a curved line from the top of the head to the shoulder.

STEP 3

There are a lot of details to be added on the face, the hands, and the feet, so take your time filling them in. Finish off your outlines by drawing tufts of hair all over the gorilla's body. Notice how the hair sticks out on the elbows.

STEP 4

Darken the eyes, nostrils, and sides of the face. Shade in the feet, hands, and far leg. Give definition to the curves in the arms and legs by shading the places where the body bends. Touch up the fur details, and erase any unwanted pencil lines. Looks like your gorilla wants a banana!

GIANT PANDA

Giant pandas are among the rarest mammals in the world. Fewer than 1,000 are left in the wild, and they live in the bamboo forests of China. Giant pandas can grow up to 6 feet tall and weigh up to 270 pounds! Habitat destruction is the greatest threat to their survival. Pandas live almost entirely on bamboo. When these forests are cut down, the panda's main food supply disappears. China's bamboo forests are now protected by law.

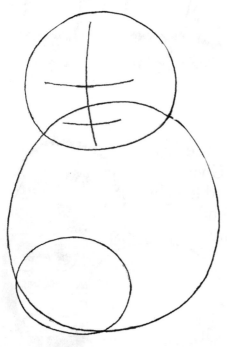

 STEP 1 This time, start by drawing a circle for the head, then adding guidelines for the face. Next, draw a larger circle for the body, intersecting the head circle. Draw a smaller circle overlapping the body on the lower left. This will be a guideline for the panda's belly.

 STEP 2 Draw oval shapes for the arms and paws on top of the body outline, as shown. Now draw one leg extending out from the side of the lower body, then draw the other leg on top of the body outline, as you did with the arms. Don't forget to sketch the ovals for the bottoms of the feet. Center the eyes, nose, mouth, and chin, using the guidelines. Draw two ears on top of the head at this step too.

STEP 3

Add fur details to the panda's entire body outline, as shown. Next, add paw pads to the bottom of the feet and claws to the feet and paws. Outline the eye patches, and add detail to the nose. Draw the lines for the bamboo leaves and stalk, so your panda has something to eat.

STEP 4

Darken all the black areas on the ears, eyes, nose, chin, arms, and legs. Keep the rest of the head, the chest, and the belly white. Shade the foot pads and darken the mouth lines. Don't forget to erase any extra pencil lines. Wow! Your panda sure is adorable!

AFRICAN ELEPHANT

The African elephant is the largest living land mammal. It can grow to be 24 feet long and 12 feet high and can weigh up to 17,000 pounds! African elephants are endangered mainly because poachers kill them for their ivory tusks. To help fight this problem, the United States has now made it illegal to import ivory into the country, hoping that if the poachers can't sell off the ivory, they'll get discouraged and stop killing the elephants.

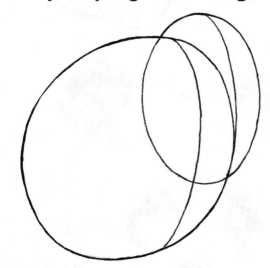

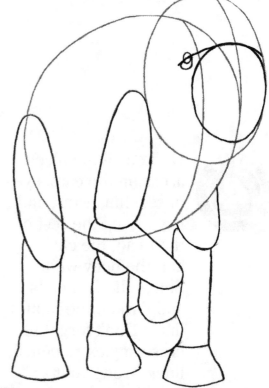

STEP 1 Now that you've mastered drawing the previous animals, try this challenging elephant. Remember to take your time and don't worry about mistakes. Begin by drawing a large circular shape for the body. Now add an oval shape for the head, which overlaps the body. Add two vertical guidelines in the head oval; notice how one of the guidelines starts and stops on the body outline.

STEP 2 Sketch oval shapes for the upper legs on the body. Draw one front leg raised at an angle, as shown. Outline a short ankle section and foot. Complete the remaining leg outlines shape by shape. Sketch a circle on the face to begin the trunk, and draw an eye, adding a line from the eye to the trunk circle.

STEP 3

Begin the trunk from the circle guideline, drawing curved lines. Using a smooth motion, outline the big ears, as shown. Sketch a curved line over the top of the elephant's face, and another under the chin. Next, draw the elephant's mouth in a V shape, as shown.

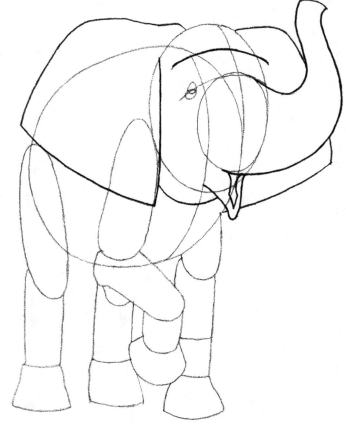

STEP 4

To give the trunk a three-dimensional shape, draw a line starting from the center of the tip to the base. Then add a few horizontal lines at the top and bottom of the trunk, as shown. Outline the tusks on either side of the mouth. Add detail lines to the face and ears. Smooth out the leg joints, and add wrinkles to the neck, knees, and ankles. Don't forget to include the rounded toes.

Finally, finish adding the details. Draw wrinkle lines on the top of the trunk where it connects to the face. Shade the areas of the ears that are closest to the head, and give definition to the edges of the ears and the tip of the trunk. Darken the eye and the inside of the mouth. Shade the areas around the tusks, the underside of the chest, and the legs that are farther away, and add a little shading between the toes. Draw background scenery if you'd like. Erase any unwanted lines, and you have yourself a mighty fine elephant!